YOUR KNOWLEDGE HAS VALUE

- We will publish your bachelor's and master's thesis, essays and papers

- Your own eBook and book - sold worldwide in all relevant shops

- Earn money with each sale

Upload your text at www.GRIN.com and publish for free

Brittany Finley

Machismo in The United States

GRIN Publishing

Bibliographic information published by the German National Library:

The German National Library lists this publication in the National Bibliography; detailed bibliographic data are available on the Internet at http://dnb.dnb.de .

This book is copyright material and must not be copied, reproduced, transferred, distributed, leased, licensed or publicly performed or used in any way except as specifically permitted in writing by the publishers, as allowed under the terms and conditions under which it was purchased or as strictly permitted by applicable copyright law. Any unauthorized distribution or use of this text may be a direct infringement of the author s and publisher s rights and those responsible may be liable in law accordingly.

Imprint:

Copyright © 2015 GRIN Verlag GmbH
Print and binding: Books on Demand GmbH, Norderstedt Germany
ISBN: 978-3-656-89319-6

This book at GRIN:

http://www.grin.com/en/e-book/289079/machismo-in-the-united-states

GRIN - Your knowledge has value

Since its foundation in 1998, GRIN has specialized in publishing academic texts by students, college teachers and other academics as e-book and printed book. The website www.grin.com is an ideal platform for presenting term papers, final papers, scientific essays, dissertations and specialist books.

Visit us on the internet:

http://www.grin.com/

http://www.facebook.com/grincom

http://www.twitter.com/grin_com

Brittany Finley

Span-101-U6-Winter Session-Online

Synthesis Module 6 Step 6

Research Topic: The effects of acculturation and immigration on substance abuse and addiction in the Latino Community.

Machismo in the United States

The word Latino will be used in this paper because of its inclusivity. It has been used in the United States by people of Hispanic and Latin decent as a means of legitimacy in politics, humanities and literature. To avoid any uncertainty, Latino, according to the Royal Academy of Spanish Language, is used to reference both males and females (Torres-Rivera 26). In the United States, Latinos are younger than the general population on average. About 60% of the US population is 39 years or younger, while over ¾ of the Latino population falls in this quotient. 21% of Latino homes fall below the poverty line. Almost 15% of all those jailed in the United States are Latino and 23% of these are drug related (27). Therefore, it is highly probable that any counselor or clinician working with Latino clients will encounter addiction and substance use or abuse.

The Latino population provides a new and complex task for professionals in addiction counseling. Latinos can no longer be classified as Mexican American, Puerto Rican, and Cuban. Over the past 20 years, the demographics have changed tremendously. The changing trend demands that substance abuse and addiction treatment method include a multi-ethnic and multi-racial perspective. Simply focusing on locality and region is no longer acceptable or effective. Clinicians must study and remain current on contemporary demographic growth, culture, cultural competency, and the accompanying treatment methods being used. (Paz 124)

The Latino community is comprised of almost 30 million people in the United States. Their definition is not a simple task, because they are not a large single entity. Their diversity now includes people from Mexico, Cuba, Puerto Rico, the Caribbean, and South and Central America. Apart from their nationality, they are made up of multiple ethnic and racial backgrounds. In American society, Latinos can include: "Yaqui Indians from the Southwest, Blacks from Puerto Rico, Venezuela, or Columbia, Mizquitas from Nicaragua, Guaranis from Paraguay and Cholos from Peru." (124)

"During an interview with Leonel Costillo, former Commissioner of the Immigration and Naturalization Service, he indicated that the old practice of forcing Spanish speaking clients to learn English was no longer viable." (124) It appears today that time and focus is spent in the reverse manner, teaching professionals to learn Spanish in hopes of achieving accommodation. This is a monumental shift in the social service standard, as their goal is no longer assimilation. This is a major societal shift also. An evaluation of acculturation and adaptation levels has replaced the more meaningful and permanent solution. (124) According to the free Merriam Webster dictionary, acculturation is the "process in which members of one cultural group adopt the beliefs and behaviors of another group." Instead of fighting xenophobia and promoting cultural acceptance, the idea of passive analysis has triumphed.

Mental health and addiction professionals must be knowledgeable and cautious when working with clients. It is imperative that people are understood to be culturally linked, and thus in order for methods of diagnosis and treatment to be effective, they absolutely must take in to consideration the culture and background of the client. It is normal today for many programs to exclude external variables as factors in substance use. One example is the neglect of machismo, "(which is related to male superiority and the ability to achieve sexual conquest and is also a combination of virtue, courage, romanticism, and fearlessness)" (28) in a 12 step program. If the approach is single or too general in its scope, it threatens to minimize individual differences, behaviors, experiences, and the ability to make any changes. In contrast, a multimodal approach may be understood and defined using a multicultural, bilingual, bicultural, and familial perspective. This would not be an approach that neglected a predisposition to substance abuse, but would enhance a diagnosis by including environmental and lifestyle influences on addiction. (28-29)

Old ideas used in Euro American treatment have shown to be ineffective when addressing Latinos, immigration and acculturation. They tend to focus on the removal survival skills such as the distrust of outsiders, and a reliability on instincts instead of logic. While this may be effective for some cultures, they are necessary skills in many Latino communities, especially those prevalent in violence and drug abuse.

"Sue, Arrendondo, and McDavis were among the first to recognize the ethical implications for counselors who do not understand the survival dynamics of Latinos in hostile environments. They recommended that the American Counseling Association develop and standardize multicultural counseling competencies for professional counselors." (Torres-Rivera 29)

The Association of Multicultural Counseling and Development (AMCD) did respond with a statement and the Substance Abuse and Mental Health Services Administration created a manual. The latter wasn't near as culturally thoughtful. (29)

As a result, the much too conservative approach, which attempts to help Latinos adjust to life by dealing with dysfunctional behavior has proven too narrow and ineffective. It has been heavily criticized for simply looking at issues like unemployment, family problems, living conditions, and so on.) A tactic that is able to look beyond the repressive is needed. (29)

An examination of acculturation is necessary in understanding addiction and substance abuse in Latinos. Its role alongside immigration is key to prevention, intervention, and ultimately treating Latino clients

"Acculturation refers to a complex set of phenomena resulting from continuous contact between groups of individuals from different cultures, including subsequent changes in the cultural patterns of one or both groups. By definition, acculturation is a process, rather than a static variable, and depends on social interaction to unfold. (Martinez Jr. 307)

Different influences including language proficiency, language use, nativity status, cultural-related behavioral preferences, and ethnic identity are great indicators of acculturation. Unfortunately, its complexity has led to various studies with wide ranging and often inconsistent findings. (Martinez Jr. 307) Despite this convolution, it can be said with some certainty that there exists a direct relationship between acculturation and the risk for substance abuse and abnormal conduct. For example, using data from the National Comorbidity Survey, Ortega et al.in 2000 studied the life-long chance for greater substance use and psychiatric disorders among Latinos, most notably Mexican American and Puerto Rican. The control accounted for similar age, income and education. The findings showed that US nativity status and English language inclination, by themselves, were able to forecast accurately the risk for substance- use disorders. (307) This is a remarkable finding itself, and one that sits at the heart of current understanding. It isn't an isolated study. Using data from the Hispanic Health and Nutrition Evaluation Survey, Amaro et. al, in 1990, using similar controls, found in US born Latinos an increased cocaine and marijuana use in contrast to foreign-born Latinos. In 1993, Vega, Gil, Warheit, Zimmerman, and Apospori showed comparable results. Acculturation influences were again directly linked with reports by adolescent Cuban boys. The controls included psychosocial and familial values. (307)

These studies are not simply productive in their ability to show present and past tendencies. They have also shown to be good predictors, which is ultimately the goal for professionals as they look for ways to better treat Latino patients. In a study done in 1998 by Vega et al., results concluded that drug abuse or dependence was 6.5 times greater for those spending 13 years or more in the US, as opposed to those spending less than 13 years. (307)It seems that as Latinos spend more time in the US, acculturation stress increases and their likelihood for developing psychological and substance abuse issues follows suit.

Acculturation stress has been described as, "a response by people to life events that are rooted in intercultural contact." (Buchanan 741) There are many factors that can trigger an escalation in acculturation stress, putting Latinos at greater risk. These stressors include differences in acculturation between parents and adolescents, language conflict, language behavior, perceived discrimination, lack of commitment to the family, and the culture of origin. (741) Family relationships are keystone of the Latino culture. Familism is a cultural value in which the family is the main source of emotional, informative and instrumental backing. Familism protects the adolescent from experiencing an adverse effect to the stresses of acculturation. Family conflict has the obvious opposite effect as it is both an instigator of stress, and a consequence. As stress increases, family conflict gets worse. Together, conflict and familism have shown to lead to the Latino adolescent's inclination to either internalize or externalize problems. While there hasn't been any specific Latino studies, looking at the general population shows that greater substance abuse comes as more problems are externalized. The odd finding comes as it was learned that the opposite is also true; higher internalizing problems is a greater indicator for calculating lower substance abuse rates. A theory developed by Elliot in 1995 combines social control theory, social learning theory, and the strain theory in order to get a better picture of those experiences that lead to delinquency and drug use. Findings show that the impact of weak bonds with the family or important positive peers combined with the strong delinquent bonds are a principal conduit to further delinquent behaviors, including drug use and abuse. One criticism of Elliot's theory is the omission of the adolescent's interpersonal characteristics, personality traits, and affective states. (743) This critical backlash is seen every time there is discussion concerning the effects of environmental factors on substance abuse. Instead of working together, often it's a tug-of-war for scholarly supremacy.

While adolescent stress due to family conflict and decreased familism has increased the risk of substance abuse, the difference in acculturation stressors and rates between parents and the Latino youth can also be a serious problem. These are called "acculturation gaps" (Martinez 308) and it increases as the amount of time spent in the US and exposure to the American culture increases. This is often called "differential acculturation" (308) Respeto, or indisputable respect for parental authority and a core value in the Latino family, quickly deteriorates as the singular and self-absorbed value system in the US takes over. Immigrant Latino parents become increasingly frustrated as they witness their authority and cultural principles undermined by outside influences, including other young delinquents. It is the old question concerning the chicken and the egg. Acculturation leads to stress for Latino youth. Instead of returning to family for support, they look elsewhere because of the acculturation gap that exists, which grows wider as a result, leading to an on and on.

Another important factor that must be discussed is perceived discrimination, which has been associated with substance abuse and violent behavior. Perception is quite important during adolescence as they begin to form their ethnic identities. Perceived discrimination can and will be disrupting as it adds confusion and shame. Shrake and Rhee discovered that perceived discrimination could be a beneficial indicator of internalizing and externalizing problems. They concluded that problematic conduct is directly related to an adolescent's perceptions of racial discrimination. Other studies have shown that adolescents of various racial backgrounds reported occurrences such as "having been called a racially insulting name, having been threatened by peers because of their race or ethnicity, and believing that they had been given a lower grade in school because of their ethnicity or race." (Okamoto 719) Discrimination is linked with distress, depression and anxiety. There haven't been many studies done explicitly looking at perceived discrimination and Latinos. There have been reports of Latino youth experiencing discrimination because of skin color, immigration concerns and language fluency. As Latinos differ from other races and cultures and their experiences, more studies should be done looking at the effects of perceived discrimination and externalizing problems, specifically.

The preceding findings definitely advocate for the implementation of programs that are specifically intended to support immigrant families while they adapt to like in the US. This adaptation often restricts the parent's ability to safeguard their children from substance use and other behavioral issues. As prevention increases, the available evidence has shown that the best programs will address acculturation stressors as a family issue rather than an individual problem. (Martinez 315)

Competency, according to the Heritage Dictionary is defined as "(1) Properly or well qualified: capable, (2) Adequate for the purpose: suitable, sufficient, (3) Legally qualified or fit: admissible." (Paz 126)

"Culturally competent substance abuse treatment service delivery refers to clinicians and agencies that demonstrate knowledge, values and skills for working with individuals from a different cultural background." Romero defined it as, "personal qualities of the care provider that are a function of personal growth and ongoing examination of one's own cultural influences, i.e., beliefs, values and attitudes and how these impact the therapeutic encounter." (126)

Cultural competence has become more popular in the last few years as a result of its ability to improve efforts of assessing current effective and competent programs with Latinos. It begins by recognizing the knowledge, values and skills that are essential for a clinician to be competent culturally. Personal experience and serious study are required in order to avoid cultural characteristics that may lend themselves to stereotypes (A common135). This is only a beginning, but studies have shown that actual damage may be done by treating Latinos without competent cultural understanding.

A common misconception in the US is that Latinos use drugs more often than whites. The evidence does not support this. Looking at available studies and evidence, it can be said that Latino youth are at a much greater risk for particular issues associated with substance use, including school failure, incarceration and mental health problems. Integration into the US results in acculturation, and as this greater assimilation occurs, so does the risk of drug use among Latinos. It is true today that many counselors, clinicians, and mental health professionals who treat Latinos with addiction problems still use simplistic approaches. These clients would and need to be better served Latino clients in the US continue to struggle in understanding how discrimination and immigration have fully affected and changed them. Substance abuse problems should be looked at as problems in living, lifestyle, and habits that have been learned as a means to survive. These problems must be "investigated, understood, and treated from the perspective of their experience as well as from the perspective of their culture." (Torres-Rivera 39) It is important that care and treatment begin at the counselor level. Once the research is done, new methods tried and tested, clinicians can begin to implement these new ideas, and real progress can begin.

It is peculiar though that at the end of it all, we realize that we are all human and quite similar. The barriers that make life difficult are simply those that we so often choose to ignore. When we do not ignore them, we find similarities and common ground. Maybe that is the scariest thing of all.

MLA Formatted Annotated Bibliography

Buchanan, Rachel Lee; Smokowski, Paul Richard. *Substance Use & Misuse*. Vol. 44 Issue 5, p740-762. 2009. Print.

>The reason for the conducted research included an examination of the relationship between acculturation stress and substance use in Latino adolescents. Interviews were conducted in the home at four different times between 2005 and 2007. Of the 286 Latinos studied, 65% were foreign born. The study pointed out that acculturation stress heavily impacted family and friend relationships, and thus adolescent mental health, ultimately leading to substance abuse. The discovered stressors found to bridge the gap between acculturation and abuse includes parent-adolescent conflict, internalizing and externalizing problems.
>
>Buchanan and Smokowski are able to take a more pointed look at the adolescent age group. Their article and research is important because it comes from first party data obtained while visiting the intended over a 2 year time frame. As 37% of the US Latino population is under the age of 19, this work is important in beginning to understand how and when it begins. It also gives counselors and future researchers a sound baseboard from which to launch their own work.
>
>This is a great article for my research and understanding of acculturation and its effects on substance abuse because the work and its fruits began in the home at a younger age. It is essential to get a good picture of family life, traditions and values. It is imperative to fully understand what separates the Latino culture from other cultures.

Martinez Jr., Charles R. *Family Relations.* Jul2006, Vol. 55 Issue 3, p306-317. Print. Jul. 2010.

The research done by Martinez studied the relationship between parent-youth differential acculturation and the likelihood of youth substance-use. It used a sample size of 73 newly immigrated Latino families with middle school aged children. Results showed that the greater the acculturation disparity between parents and youth, the greater the chance of substance use. Also, it was learned that the greater the acculturation, the more stress in the family which led to degenerating parenting practices. Martinez determined that future policies and practices must deal with acculturation as a family process, not simply a single psychological issue. Martinez also uses multiple agents when conducting his research.

Martinez is able to show direct effects of acculturation on the family, and in turn, the consequences that these effects have on Latino youth and their increased likelihood of substance use and abuse. Also, and maybe more importantly, he is able to use these results to make a case for new policy; one that includes acculturation in the family dynamic instead of letting it be treated as an isolated problem. Also, the research was compiled using more than one researcher, increasing the accuracy of his findings.

I liked this article because it related Latino youth, Latino families, acculturation, and the need for a change in strategy. Its recognition that intervention should be refocused from pursuing acculturation to addressing family environmental stress and disruptions in parenting, has been useful for my research because of its practical use in the real world. Many have adopted this viewpoint in their work already. By realizing that acculturation leads to particular stressors, it allows counselors and researchers to maximize their time and efforts on more impactful areas. So, I used this article to refocus my work also.

Okamoto, Janet; Ritt-Olson, Anamara; Soto, Daniel; Baezconde-Garbanati, Lourdes; Unger, Jennifer B. *American Journal of Health Behavior.* Vol. 33 Issue 6, p718-727. Print. Nov/Dec. 2009

The point of this article was to observe perceived discrimination and substance use among Latino high school students. This study used 1332 self-reports of perceived discrimination and substance use behavior. This is important. It was found that Latino adolescents with higher perceived discrimination are at a much higher risk of substance use. Thus, the findings alone indicate that if the Latinos youth can get help with learning how to cope with these perceptions, it would help in preventing future substance use and abuse.

This study targets self- worth and self- perception. It includes low self-esteem, depressive symptoms, acculturative stress and psychological conflicts, as well as anxiety. While other studies may focus on families or culture, this includes the internal effects. The important thing to note is that it doesn't matter whether the discrimination is real or perceived; it is experienced and effective either way.

This article is a must for my research because it delves into something very important. When children are young, they begin to build their identities. Minorities will have a difficult time finding one that is comfortable. Add in language barriers, cultural differences etc. and it becomes much more difficult. Now, consider the fact that perceived discrimination can be very damaging to an adolescent. For me, this is a dynamic finding because it allows counselors and researchers to target one's perception at a young age, instead of simply focusing on discrimination itself.

Paz, Juan. *Journal of Human Behavior in the Social Environment.* Vol. 5 Issue ¾, p123.-137. Print. 2002.

The population of Latinos in the United States is quite complex and multi-faceted. Latinos are vigorous, lively and mobile. They live in almost every one of the fifty states. The author has determined that Clinicians who treat Latinos must deal with a complex set of environmental and systemic factors that will have a direct bearing on both the problem and the recovery. The findings suggest that treatment needs to start by systematically evaluating the cultural fit between clinicians and clients.

This study is important because it targets the clinicians themselves. Many issues including cultural competence, knowledge/conocimiento, child welfare, values, skills, and family evaluation are delved into. The study determines that it is vital to train the clinician properly before they can become competent to help the Latino community. It is a necessity to understand acculturation and adaptation, demographic growth, and migration patterns. It is stressed that Latino's, in particular, have unique needs and clinicians must be either from the community or have a deep understanding in order to obtain the skills necessary to treat the Latino community.

This article is a bit narrower in its scope. Again, though, I chose it because it focuses on something different, the clinician. In its focus, it explores in some depth, the Latino culture and acculturation while making a case that a specifically trained clinician is imperative to recovery. I tend to agree, though it will be some time before this occurs because Latinos are spread out across the US. It is difficult to find the very best Clinicians in each and every case.

Torres-Rivera, Edil; Wilbur, Michael P; Phan, Loan T; Maddux, Cleborne D; Roberst-Wilbur, Janice. *Journal of Addictions & Offender Counseling.* Vol 25 Issue 1, p26-42. Print. Oct2004.

This article is broad in its scope. It presents various different approaches that are constructed upon multicultural interventions and sociopolitical themes that offer interventions when dealing with Latinos that suffer from substance abuse issues. The different methods include multimodal interventions, multicultural approaches, and humanistic counseling from a common or basic perspective. The purpose of this is to avoid a singular narrow-minded approach that is so commonly used by many in the field.

This article is quite relevant because it drives home the complexity of the Latino culture and its demands for proper perspective when creating effective methods. It is determined that substance abuse problems may also be referred to as lifestyle or problems in living that are related to individual emotions or behaviors. Substance abuse problems or lifestyle issues find their roots in racism and discrimination in the United States. The substance abuse and dishonesty have been determined to be symptomatic coping behaviors.

I found this article to be the best research for my initial broad perspective. It encompasses many ideas found in other studies, as it concludes that a multifaceted approach is required for effective treatment. I do agree that substance abuse problems need to be investigated, understood, and treated from the perception of their involvement as well as from the viewpoint of their culture. I am often referencing this study as I begin to put the pieces together.